The Campus History Series

UNIVERSITY OF CENTRAL ARKANSAS

FRONT COVER: Old Main is the most visibly recognizable building on the campus of University of Central Arkansas (UCA). This picture captures students on the steps in 1965. While sit-ins and protests were breaking out on college campuses across the United States, UCA looks peaceful and picturesque. (Courtesy of the University of Central Arkansas Archives.)

BACKGROUND: Taken on the eve of World War II, this 1939 aerial view of campus shows UCA's humble beginnings and also how much room the campus had to grow. The empty fields were used to grow crops to stock the cafeteria. Today, UCA has expanded, and the fields have given way to recreation centers, cutting-edge athletic facilities, residence halls, and numerous buildings that house classes. (Courtesy of the University of Central Arkansas Archives.)

The Campus History Series

UNIVERSITY OF CENTRAL ARKANSAS

Dr. Vaughn Scribner and Dr. Marcus Witcher
with Phi Alpha Theta
Introduction by Dr. Houston Davis, President

Copyright © 2020 by Vaughn Scribner and Marcus Witcher with Phi Alpha Theta
ISBN 978-1-4671-0427-2

Published by Arcadia Publishing
Charleston, South Carolina

Printed in the United States of America

Library of Congress Control Number: 2019940831

For all general information, please contact Arcadia Publishing:
Telephone 843-853-2070
Fax 843-853-0044
E-mail sales@arcadiapublishing.com
For customer service and orders:
Toll-Free 1-888-313-2665

Visit us on the Internet at www.arcadiapublishing.com

*This book is dedicated to Jimmy Bryant,
who has devoted his life to preserving UCA's history.*

Contents

Acknowledgments		6
Introduction		7
1.	Campus Construction	9
2.	Student Life	53
3.	Sports	87
4.	Outreach	105

Acknowledgments

First and foremost, the authors would like to thank all of the University of Central Arkansas's students, faculty, and staff—past and present—for making our university such a vibrant, welcoming, and dynamic place in which to live, learn, and grow. Jimmy Bryant, director of the UCA Archives, was absolutely critical for this book. President Davis consulted his historical writings and documents in drafting this book's introduction, as did students when writing the subsequent chapters. Bryant's knowledge of UCA's history and his willingness to help students and faculty are unmatched. We would also like to thank the two staff members at the UCA Archives, Heather Reinold and Iain Montgomery, for aid in finding and scanning documents. Pres. Houston Davis went above and beyond in supporting the book, as did UCA Alumni Association and the chair of the Department of History, Dr. Wendy Lucas. Finally, we would like to thank the editorial staff at Arcadia Publishing for guiding us through the process.

Unless otherwise noted, all images appear courtesy of the University of Central Arkansas Archives.

INTRODUCTION

The University of Central Arkansas was founded in 1907 as the Arkansas State Normal School with the primary goal of training students to become professional Arkansas teachers. As superintendent of Arkansas schools at that time, John James Doyne authored the legislation that became Act 317 of 1907 and created the school. Doyne, who became the university's first president in 1908, never could have imagined how the school would evolve over the next century, how many lives would be changed by the opportunity to learn, or how many important milestones this esteemed university in the heart of the state would celebrate.

Soon after the school was created, one of the first orders of business was to choose a location for the campus. The brand-new, seven-member board of trustees received proposals from various cities across the state. In *The Centennial History of the University of Central Arkansas*, former UCA archivist Jimmy Bryant wrote that in order to be considered, cities had to donate at least 20 acres of land and at least $15,000. Conway, just 30 miles north of Little Rock, won with a donation of $51,753 and the choice of three tracts of land, the largest of which was 80 acres.

From the beginning, the Conway community has played a vital role in UCA's growth and success. It is a vibrant, engaged city that is focused on progress and innovation. Nicknamed the "City of Colleges," today Conway is home to UCA and two other colleges, Hendrix College and Central Baptist College, both of which are private institutions of higher learning.

In "The Centennial History of the University of Central Arkansas," Bryant wrote that classes at UCA began in the fall of 1908 with nine academic departments, one building on 80 acres, 107 students and seven faculty members. Two faculty members taught in two departments, and President Doyne taught pedagogy and Latin.

"According to the 1908 'Normal Bulletin,' there were five conditions of appointment that all prospective students had to meet: '(1) At least sixteen years of age; (2) In good health; (3) Of good moral character; (4) Completed the State Course of Study or its equivalent; (5) Obligated to teach in schools of State for at least two years after graduation,'" Bryant wrote. He goes on to say that the only degree offered by the school from 1908 to 1920 was a two-year degree known as the Licentiate of Instruction (LI).

In 1925, the school's name changed to Arkansas State Teachers College. Though subtle, the name change more accurately reflected the main program of instruction and the school's mission. For decades to follow, Arkansas State Teachers College was known for its reputable Arkansas teacher-training program.

According to the University of Central Arkansas Archives, by 1967, the mission of Arkansas State Teachers College was beginning to evolve. Though teacher training was still integral to the institution's mission, other fields began to expand in liberal arts and health care. To recognize the institution's increasing academic diversity, in January of that year, Arkansas State Teachers College became State College of Arkansas.

Over the next eight years, State College of Arkansas grew rapidly and began to offer a wide range of degree programs. President Silas Snow, who supported the name change in 1967 and for whom the Snow Fine Arts Center on campus is named, prepared State College of Arkansas for the fourth and final name change. In January 1975, the Arkansas Department of Higher Education recommended the State College of Arkansas be known as the University of Central Arkansas (UCA). Former Arkansas governor David Pryor signed the bill into law on January 21, 1975, with a pen labeled "SCA has earned university status," wrote Bryant.

Today, UCA has a student body of almost 11,000 and around 1,400 full-time faculty and staff. The university offers more than 160 degrees and certificates, including technical certificates, undergraduate degrees, master's degrees, and doctoral degrees. The campus includes more than 120 buildings and facilities on more than 350 acres. UCA students typically represent all of Arkansas' 75 counties, almost all 50 states, and more than 70 foreign countries.

From its earliest beginnings as a training ground for teachers, UCA has been home to builders, dreamers, and visionaries, all intent on making a big impact in the world. UCA strives to lead with academic vitality, integrity, and diversity, and the university is proud to provide an education to many first-generation college students in the state.

While UCA is still dedicated to training excellent teachers through the College of Education, many of its other colleges and programs have seen tremendous growth and success over the years. For instance, UCA trains hundreds of health care professionals in the College of Health and Behavioral Sciences each year. These students obtain an interprofessional education in state-of-the-art clinical settings. They often go on to practice in the state and help fill a great need for well-trained nurses, health care, and medical professionals.

UCA is also dedicated to fine and performing arts and giving students in these programs first-class artistic experiences and education. Some of the university's most notable accomplishments in the arts include founding the Arkansas Shakespeare Theatre, which is the only professional Shakespeare repertory company in the state; progressing toward All-Steinway school status; and offering acclaimed courses and terminal graduate programs one can only find at UCA, including the state's only degree in film production.

In the field of technology, UCA's cyber range was the first in the region that was built for students and the first in the country that is used to teach both college and K–12 students. UCA's cutting-edge cybersecurity degree is designed to produce graduates who can identify and combat cybercrime.

Throughout its 112 years, UCA has celebrated many significant milestones and victories. In the following pages, you will learn more about those milestones as UCA's unique story is told through historic photographs and documents. The book is comprised of four chapters: Campus Construction, Student Life, Sports, and Outreach. While this is not a complete history of UCA, this volume recognizes some of the important events, traditions, buildings, and individuals that made the university what it is today.

We invite you to take a stroll down memory lane and celebrate the big moments of this prestigious university in the center of the state. For more than a century, UCA has been a vital part of the city of Conway and the State of Arkansas. We hope to continue opening eyes and changing lives for generations to come.

Go Bears!

One

CAMPUS CONSTRUCTION

From its humble beginnings in the 1907 state legislature, UCA has been through four official designations and has grown to be the second-largest university in Arkansas. The Arkansas State Normal School was created to provide training for teachers who had no consistent standard of education. John J. Doyne's successful recruitment campaign quickly increased student enrollment. Initially, the school's only degree was the licentiate of instruction. In 1925, when the school adopted the name Arkansas State Teachers College, the campus had seven buildings. In time, construction flourished with the addition of the auditorium, Physical Education Building, two new residence halls, the National Youth Administration Building, and the Home Management House. This boom grew out of the Works Progress Administration (WPA) and other New Deal federal funding programs. Only Torreyson Library's 1929 construction was conducted during this time with no federal funding. When the construction of the new library was completed, it had a capacity to hold nearly 300,000 volumes. In 1913, Doyne Hall was the only residence hall on campus and was limited to female students. Today, UCA has nine on-campus residence halls and apartment complexes, with more off-campus school-affiliated housing options. More campus growth came with the development of the College of Business, Bear Hall, and Donaghey Hall. In 2019, Pres. Houston Davis announced a $20 million gift for the construction of the Windgate Center for Fine and Performing Arts, which will be one of the most state-of-the-art facilities in Arkansas. It will contain interior and exterior art facilities, a new art gallery, a concert hall, and studio and classroom space.

Also in 2019, UCA broke ground on a new 80,000-square-foot Integrated Health Sciences Building. The facility will be home to the School of Nursing and the Department of Communication Sciences and Disorders, along with the Nabholz Center for Healthcare Simulation and an Interprofessional Teaching Center to be utilized by the entire college. The facility will further enhance UCA's role as a health education leader and innovator in meeting the health care needs of the state and region.

—Jacalyn Pearce
undergraduate, History

Science Building, State Normal School, Conway, Ark.

The Arkansas State Normal School's Science Building, the first building on campus, housed the first classes. This picture was taken only five years after the school's founding, when ASNS had only nine academic departments. The building was later named for Everett E. Cordrey. Cordrey started teaching science classes at ASNS in 1914 and later took on the role of dean of instruction, which he held until his 1950 retirement.

Doyne Hall, the second major building on campus, was the first dormitory on campus in 1913; until then, students lived with Conway residents. Doyne was named after the school's first president, John J. Doyne, who taught Latin and pedagogy in the classroom, in addition to his administrative duties, until his resignation in 1917. Housing 100 women initially, Doyne Hall later hosted the men's dormitory.

An aerial view of the campus in 1920 focuses on what was known at the time as the Administration Building. This building was erected in 1919 at a cost of $107,000. Former Arkansas governor George Donaghey headed the construction and chose redbrick and Batesville marble. The familiar circular drive is visible next to the open fields where future buildings eventually emerged.

Taken in 1929, this photograph shows the Green Building, which was designed not only to train teachers but also to model a rural schoolhouse. Even though the model school was known as the "Practice, Training, and Demonstration School," the building was always called the "Green Building" by students and faculty because of its green-colored wood.

Men dig the trench at the ground-breaking ceremony for the original library, Torreyson Library. Named for UCA's second president, W.B. Torreyson, the library was located next to the Administration Building. Torreyson Library was built in 1929 without any federal funds thanks to J.J. Hiegel of the Hiegel Lumber Company, who waited years for compensation because of the economic crash at the beginning of the Great Depression.

This 1933 aerial photograph shows a considerable amount of expansion on the campus. Focusing on the rear of the Administration Building, the relatively new library can be seen on the right, along with an additional five buildings. The empty fields behind the Administration Building are actually garden plots given to students to maintain crops of their choice to supply the school cafeteria.

In 1933, this was the Torreyson Library, though the building is now known as Harrin Hall. Today, Harrin Hall is home to academic advising, financial aid, veterans' services, and the registrar's office. It is one of the oldest-remaining buildings on campus.

This 1939 photograph shows the building that housed ASTC's training school, where students taught local elementary children as preparation for their careers. The training school was built in 1925 because the Green Building was no longer large enough to accommodate the number of children enrolled in the teacher education program.

This is a photograph of McAlister Hall with trees lining the drive toward the Administration Building. McAlister Hall was named after UCA's most popular president, Col. Heber L. McAlister, who resigned his presidency in order to accompany his Army Reserves regiment to Alaska during World War II. The building was constructed toward the end of the Hoover Administration with money from the Reconstruction Finance Corporation; it became the new women's dormitory, which allowed Doyne Hall to become the first men's dormitory.

This 1940 picture demonstrates the changes to Doyne Hall; it was initially a dormitory for women, then later men. Eventually, the original building was torn down to make way for a new building, which currently houses the health sciences programs.

This 1945 photograph of the Cordrey Science Building shows a three-story building with dormer windows that will look familiar even to recent students. The Science Building housed the natural sciences, the school's first library, and four large classrooms.

Changes to campus can be easily seen in this photograph of Wingo Hall with cars parked out front. Wingo Hall was named for Sen. Otis T. Wingo. The building started out as a men's dormitory before being remodeled to accommodate its current occupants: UCA's administrative offices. Students today will envy the convenient parking that was once available on campus.

Firefighters put out the blaze that destroyed the training school in 1947. The structure had been used since the 1920s to train teachers in a model rural schoolhouse.

This 1950 aerial image shows growth across the UCA campus. McAlister Hall and Nolen Irby Elementary School are visible in front of the Administration Building and the circle, and the track ring is visible where the football field is currently located. The individual plots given to students to contribute food to the cafeteria are gone, but parking in front of buildings is still widely available.

By 1949, the Green Building was still in use for modeling a type of rural schoolhouse that students would eventually work in. Built around 1912, the Green Building was the third building on campus. Over time, the school added a number of disciplines as it moved away from its initial focus as a teacher-training school. The Green Building was torn down in 1962 to make room for the new Torreyson Library.

The Nolen Irby Elementary School educated the children of returning veterans of World War II. Nolen Irby was located on campus so that parents could more easily complete their own education. Seen here is a group of children playing out front in approximately 1947. By 1962, the elementary school program ended in order to use the classroom space for the growing student body.

The "Corner Town" Veteran Housing consisted of a number of small houses built to support the massive growth in veteran student enrollment in the postwar years. Enrollment jumped from 300 in 1945 to more than 1,400 by 1950. These simple cottages hardly made a dent in the desperate need for housing. Besides Corner Town, many veterans lived in small trailers on the edge of campus. Despite President Irby's and Colonel McAlister's efforts, some students were turned away because of a lack of housing.

Bernard Hall was built in 1939 with money from Pres. Franklin D. Roosevelt's New Deal. It was named after Mary Augusta Bernard, a professor of drawing and penmanship. Bernard eventually became the head of the Department of Art, which she retained until her death in 1933. By the early 1950s, when this photograph was taken, the building was already recognizable in its most current form.

The Veterans Infirmary was constructed in 1948 from the excess war budget. It was used until 1955, when the massive influx of post–World War II veterans finally assimilated into the student body. After 1955, both men and women were treated in the clinic, but only women were allowed beds in the infirmary.

Seen here in 1953, Doyne Hall was still going strong after 40 years as a dormitory. In 1975, the dormitory was torn down, and the Doyne Health Science Center was built in the same location. Today, the Doyne Health Science Center houses the nursing and psychology programs.

This photograph of the Administrative Building was taken from the street, which obscures the view of the circular drive. Pictured are the brick columns, erected by the classes of 1924 and 1925. For students today, possibly the most striking detail is the lack of parked cars lining the drive. Their absence makes for a picturesque view of the campus's most important building.

The original Torreyson Library, built in 1929, was still functioning as the campus library in 1957, with convenient parking right outside the building. Today, the building has been renamed Harrin Hall and holds academic advising, financial aid, veterans' services, and the registrar's office.

Baridon Hall, built in 1940, housed the school's music program until the Department of Music moved to the newly built Snow Fine Arts Center in 1968. In 1992, Dr. Win Thompson led the extensive renovations to transform the building into a dormitory.

Construction of Minton Hall in 1958 added another dormitory to campus. The building was named for Hubert L. Minton, who became the head of the geography department in 1927. He was well known for his work with public relations and extension services. Before the building was razed in 2010, Minton Hall served as the Residential College for the College of Liberal Arts.

The funding for construction of the Student Center in 1958 originated with student fees, as this sign advertised. Later, President Farris worked to increase the activities available to students in order to avoid the stereotype of being a "suitcase college" (i.e., a college without a vibrant student culture).

PRESIDENT'S HOME

The President's Home, shown here in 1960, was originally built during the Great Depression with a Public Works Administration (PWA) grant and a low-interest loan from the federal government. This house has hosted every president since Col. Heber McAlister, who was president at the time of its construction in 1937.

Short Hall was named for Gilbert Young Short, who obtained the licentiate of instruction in 1912; he taught for a year before becoming the school's registrar from 1916 until his retirement in 1953. Short Hall was a dormitory, as shown here in 1960. The increasing number of dormitories correlates to the growing student population.

The Physical Education Building was renamed in honor of Jeff Farris Sr. after his death in 1961. His son Jeff Farris Jr. also held a doctorate of philosophy in health and physical education and took over the department after his father's death. In 1975, Farris Jr. became president of the newly named University of Central Arkansas.

Similar to the view of the Administration Building only six years earlier, this photograph shows cars parked parallel to the drive in the grass. More drastic changes to what would eventually become known as Alumni Drive came much later in the campus's evolution.

The construction of the new Torreyson Library took place where the old Green Building once stood. This cutting-edge building could hold 1,200,000 books in 1969 and contained a soundproofed typing room, water fountains, and restrooms, none of which had been present in the original library building.

This view shows the newly completed Torreyson Library, which looks similar to its present-day iteration, aside from the most recent facade changes. Torreyson Library became one of the first libraries in Arkansas to fully integrate computer technology into its library management system.

W.C. Ferguson was dean of the college under Pres. A.J. Meadors and served until his death in 1954. The position he once occupied is now known as the provost. In 2013, the Ferguson Chapel was added to the National Register of Historic Places.

Construction of the Christian Cafeteria, which began in 1962, was completed by 1963. The new cafeteria was named for Elizabeth L. Christian, who served as an associate professor of home economics until 1930. Before the Christian Cafeteria's construction, the commons, eventually named McCastlain Hall, contained the dining hall and student lounge.

The Buffalo Alumni Hall was established in 1995 with money donated from Harvey A. Buffalo, a UCA alum who spent his career with the US Foreign Service before becoming an entrepreneur. The UCA Alumni Association hosts tailgating activities at UCA football home games, as well as group travel opportunities. It also provides member privileges at the library; Health, Physical Education and Recreation (HPER) fitness center; and discounts at the UCA Bookstore and a number of other stores around Conway and online.

The Harding Centennial Plaza was a gift from Rush Harding III, a UCA alum and board of trustees member. Then-president Lu Hardin's wife, Mary, designed the fountain and plaza, which was constructed in 2005 and dedicated in 2006. The fountain is now a beautiful campus focal point, providing a scenic backdrop for pictures and ceremonies, as well as for student pep rallies and gatherings.

Between Irby Hall and the Torreyson Library is the Irby courtyard, a large open space with benches where students can study outside or meet with friends. This area was constructed in 1992 to replace the earlier Nolen Irby Elementary School that had been on campus since 1949. Irby is home to the College of Liberal Arts, which contains six departments and more than 800 students.

The Jefferson D. Farris (Jr.) Honors Hall was named for UCA's sixth president, who served from 1975 to 1986. The Farris Honors Hall is the location of the UCA Schedler Honors College, which was established by Dr. Norbert Schedler in 1982, during President Farris's tenure. Students in the honors college maintain a 3.5 grade point average and complete an honors thesis.

Wingo Hall, built in 1934 as part of Pres. Franklin D. Roosevelt's New Deal, was named for Sen. Otis T. Wingo, who submitted the legislation that established the original Arkansas State Normal School. Initially, Wingo Hall served as a dormitory for men whose rent paid the building's construction loans. Today, Wingo Hall functions as the school's administrative center, containing the offices of the president and provost and the meeting room of the board of trustees.

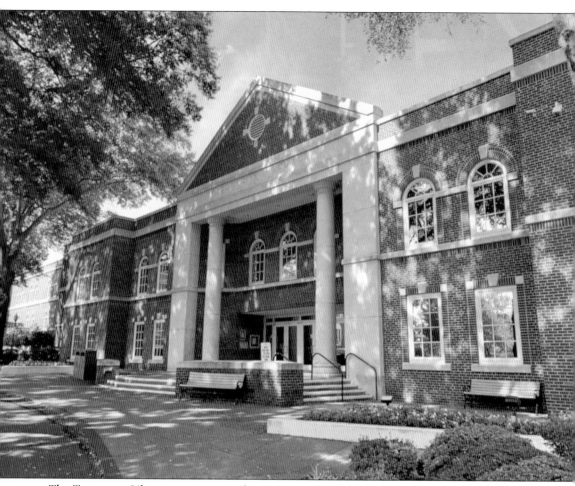

The Torreyson Library continues to be an integral part of the UCA campus. The library has served more than 400,000 students in person and online, providing access to 145 databases, more than 60 study rooms, and a Starbucks coffee shop, plus tutoring and printing services for students and faculty.

The UCA Student Center has played an important role in transforming the university into a vibrant community with a variety of events hosted by the student government association and a number of student organizations. Recently renovated, the Student Center has a ballroom that can hold more than 500 people at a time.

The Snow Fine Arts Center opened in 1968 and was named for UCA's longest-serving president, Silas D. Snow, who served from 1953 until 1975. He saw the school through two of its name changes and considered the school's newly conferred university status to be his greatest achievement. This building currently accommodates the Department of Music, the UCA Community School of Music, and the theatre department.

Constructed in 2013, this building houses the College of Business. This state-of-the-art facility contains a dozen classrooms with tiered seating; an auditorium, which seats 168 students; faculty offices; and a coffee shop. The college is home to more than a dozen different undergraduate and graduate programs, including Arkansas's only insurance and risk management degree. There are more than 1,500 students enrolled, many of whom participate in the college's extensive internship program to gain crucial work experience and networking connections. Graduates frequently gain employment with companies like Acxiom, Dillard's, Walmart, and J.B. Hunt Transport, among others. UCA's College of Business has been and will continue to be one of Arkansas's leading programs.

The Conway Corporation Center for Sciences was completed in 2017 with donations from Conway Corporation, the city's public utilities entity. The cutting-edge building houses the College of Natural Sciences and Mathematics, which offers classes in physics, engineering, microbiology, and genetics and faculty research laboratories. These laboratories are equipped with technology that students will encounter on the job, which means their UCA education will give graduates an advantage in entering the workforce.

Donaghey Hall is UCA's newest residence hall, but it also provides commercial offices on the ground floor, with three floors of apartments for 165 upperclassmen residents. Donaghey Hall is located on the corner of Donaghey Avenue and Bruce Street. Current businesses in the mixed-use space include Einstein Bros. Bagels, Marble Slab Creamery, Great American Cookies, Twisted Taco, the UCA Makerspace, and the UCA Welcome Center.

The HPER (Health, Physical Education, and Recreation) Building first opened in 2000 to provide faculty and students with a space for exercise and recreation. In 2012, UCA added a six-lane swimming pool, group exercise classrooms, new weights, and cardio rooms. The basketball courts were refinished as part of the renovations, which also added windows overlooking the nearby Jewel E. Moore Nature Preserve.

Two

STUDENT LIFE

As one of the oldest universities in the state, the University of Central Arkansas has a rich history that has been shaped and influenced by the student body since 1907. The faculty and administration at UCA have welcomed student expression in a variety of forms, which has led to activism and inclusiveness in student life, making the UCA experience unique from any other university in Arkansas. *The Echo* has been the voice of the student body since 1909, and has continuously tried to widen its content, boldly tying together student issues with national and international events, while opening the door for platforms like KUCA and the *Vortex* to emerge. What started as "the Dramatic Club" in 1920, later known as "Little Theatre," has grown immensely and transformed UCA into one of the strongest theatre schools in the state, creating shows that attract a broad audience. Students supported war efforts through the Women's Auxiliary Corps (WAC), Branch No. 3, during World War II, which allowed more than 1,800 men to enter combat. During the 1990s, students became increasingly engaged in local and national politics through Young Democrats and Young Republicans. More recently, students canvassed and hosted voter-registration drives for the 2016 and 2018 elections. Platforms like the PRISM Alliance have built supportive communities for minority groups on campus, while groups such as the debate club have allowed students to challenge one another. Finally, UCA's storied Greek life allows a diverse set of students to engage with each other and their community. The students who attend UCA not only define and enrich their own experience through the four years they spend on campus but also create opportunities for generations ahead.

—Riley Kovalcheck and George "Trace" Rhode
undergraduates, History and Business Administration

The Echo is a weekly student-published newspaper and was established in 1909. Under faculty advisor Roberta Clay, editor Jack Shelton and his staff of columnists and reporters won first place in 1950 from the Columbia Scholastic Press Association for the third year in a row. In 1949, the Arkansas College Press Association gave Shelton and his staff the General Excellence Award at its annual Convention. Beginning in 1950, the newspaper was published every Wednesday.

The first *Scroll* was published in 1915, but by 1949, the *Scroll* still only had a staff of 10 students. The staff worked throughout the academic school year to build an annual for student consumption. Each student was given a specific section or task throughout the year, such as photographing for the *Scroll* or covering the Greek life community on campus.

Ciama was a scholarship society in the early days of UCA. Its goals were to promote academic achievement and bonds between its members. It was one of the first societies for women (now known as sororities). Later renamed Sigma Tau Theta, it was next chartered by Sigma Sigma Sigma and is still active on campus.

Formed in 1917, the Owls responded to the demand for a different experience than the current literary societies and clubs offered. Their main goal was to offer young men the chance to gain experience operating inside a formally organized body, as well as with parliamentary procedure. The Owls was restricted to only 20 members and only to juniors and seniors.

The boys' debate club, under the direction of Coach Dean Depew McBrien, created a record of victories. The organization called themselves the "Windmills" because a small gold windmill was awarded to those who won a place on the team. The Windmills claimed to have achieved perfection in the 1924 school year, where "supporters and friends marvel[ed] at a defeat." Club members aimed to promote the interest of debating regionally and traveled during the second year throughout Arkansas, Oklahoma, and Louisiana to compete.

Maude Carmichael created and led the women's debate club in 1924. Carmichael and the club members organized in hopes of being able to "engage in mental combat" with girls in other colleges across the state but were unfortunately unable to secure opponents. Despite their lack of competition, the club stayed together in hopes that women would be able to find willing opponents in future years.

The Dramatic Club was founded in 1920 and quickly started performing regularly. That year, *The Three Chauffeurs* was performed in February and *Miss Somebody Else* in May. All of the club's proceeds went to the stage fund. Miss Kirkland led the club and told *The Scroll* that the students "showed a willingness at all times to do their part and maintain a high standard."

Despite not being Greek organizations, literary societies and clubs hosted similar activities to current fraternities and sororities. One such activity was a formal banquet hosted by the Crestomath and Wingo societies pictured above. Modern-day fraternities and sororities host regular formals, which provide the opportunity to wear formal attire and dance.

Student designations, such as 1928's "prettiest girl," Mildred Robinson, remained firmly tethered to fraternity and sorority life in the first half of the 20th century. Other awardees in 1928 included "best all-round girl" (Lois Hamm) and "*Scroll* sponsor" (Clyde Runyan). Eventually, such awards extended to men and are critical facets of modern-day homecoming ceremonies.

In 1930, students elected various "favorites" among their colleagues, including "most ideal college students," "biggest school booster," "prettiest girl and most handsome boy," "most representative athlete," "most popular students," and "our favorite entertainer." Pictured are Elizabeth Watson and Alton Thomas—"most ideal college students"—and Lillie Taylor, "our favorite entertainer."

Academics have always been important to fraternity and sorority members at UCA. Here, a group of coeds studies at the ASTC library in 1941.

In March 1943, a total of 249 women arrived as the first class of the Women's Auxiliary Corps, Branch No. 3, at ATSC. The purpose of the WAC was to use women in noncombative roles, allowing more men to enter combat. Branch No. 3 trained more than 1,800 women alone, but by 1945 almost 100,000 women were serving in the WAC across the nation. This allowed almost 100,000 men to join the war.

While the WAC was stationed at UCA, one of its members, Pvt. Helen Kent, was awarded the Distinguished Flying Cross and the Air Medal with three oak leaf clusters in honor of her husband, Lt. Earl Kent. Lieutenant Kent and his crew had participated in 20 bombing missions over enemy-occupied Europe before they were shot down and listed as missing in action on March 31, 1943. To properly honor Lieutenant Kent, the US Army Air Forces conducted an awards ceremony at Estes Stadium on October 22, 1943, which more than 3,000 attended. As the ceremony was taking place, nine twin-engine aircraft from Stuttgart Army Airfield flew over in close formation. After Private Kent completed her training at WAC, Branch No. 3, she was sent to New Guinea and rose to the rank of sergeant.

The Women's Auxiliary Corps members typically ranged in age from 21 to 45, but the average age was 26. The WAC put the "miss into missions." Many of the women had completed their master's or doctorates but felt responsible to contribute to the war efforts. Throughout World War II, women realized that a "total war effort" meant women's help was needed to win.

Members of the WAC not only contributed to the war effort but also made local history as the first women to patrol the streets of Little Rock. The WAC worked with the Army Military Police. Further, according to the *Log Cabin Democrat*, the first women to fly in military formation were members of Women's Auxiliary Corps, Branch No. 3, flying from Conway to Stuttgart.

Before there was a homecoming queen, which started at ASTC in 1946, there was the *Scroll* queen. In 1945, the *Scroll* queen was Margie Brown, member of Alpha Sigma Alpha. UCA's homecoming week is still closely associated with Greek life.

The 1957 UCA freshman class officers, Larry Morgan (president), Jimmy Hinton (vice president), Betty Ferris (secretary), and Linda Bush (treasurer), pose on campus.

The Four Jacks were a vocal quartet composed of ASTC students who served as musical ambassadors for the college. The group had a recording contract with Hi Records and did background work for other artists. They won first place honors in the vocal division at the Arkansas Livestock Show Talent Contest in the fall of 1958. The Four Jacks performed at other colleges in the state, a hairdresser's convention, and at a party for Little Rock businessmen and appeared on both Little Rock and Memphis television stations.

By 1964, new organizations included Delta Zeta Sorority, Pi Kappa Alpha fraternity (formerly Chi Nu), and Theta Xi fraternity. These groups were welcomed with open arms, and the first two mentioned are still active on campus to this day. In 1964, moreover, Dianna Arey, a junior from Benton, was selected as the National Sweetheart for Phi Lambda Chi fraternity.

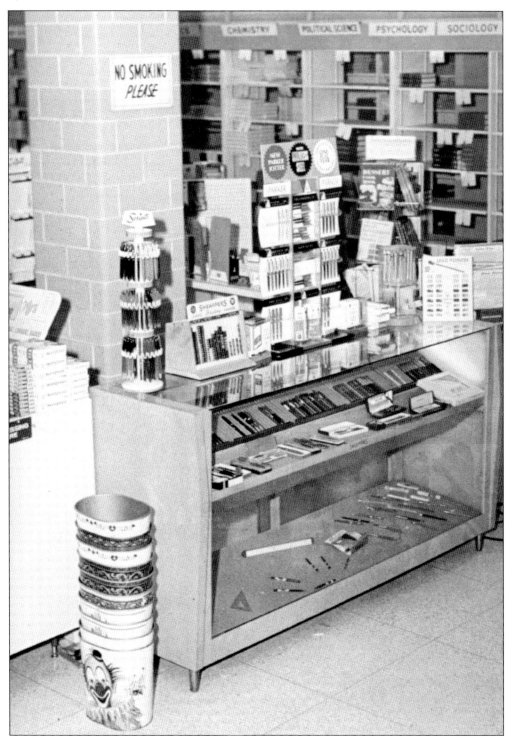
An integral part of student life on any college campus is the student bookstore. Here, in 1965, the ASTC bookstore sported a wide variety of goods, ranging from Scripto pens to textbooks and, for some odd reason, clown trash cans.

Students, faculty, and staff rely upon UCA's campus post office daily; in 1970, they did the same. Here, Elizabeth Carter is helping Nynonne Lasater mail a letter.

One of the most significant and probably most important changes to the Greek system was the addition of black fraternities and sororities. Starting with Omega Phi Mu and Omega Psi Phi in 1972, these Greek organizations gave a home in Greek life to students who had long been denied a place in the Greek system. In a reflection of changing civil rights, Omega Phi Mu sponsored Black History Week events and exhibits on campus. Pictured from left to right are Normal Gilchrest and Robert Tiswell interacting with a Black History Week exhibit.

Omega Phi Mu was the first fraternity founded on UCA's campus to expressly promote black culture and be comprised of primarily African American students. Over the next several years, more and more African American fraternities would be established at UCA. Here, members of Omega Phi Mu cheer on the Bears basketball team in 1972.

In a similar fashion to Omega Phi Mu, Alpha Kappa Alpha and Delta Sigma Theta were formed at UCA in 1975 to give young African American women a role in the Greek scene. In their first year on campus, they made Thanksgiving baskets for the community, assisted with a muscular dystrophy fund, and assisted a local daycare.

The 1974 Arkansas Model United Nations Conference was another record-breaking year and had more than 500 students in attendance. Sen. J.W. Fulbright addressed the conference.

KUCA is a student-run, commercial-free radio station that began in 1976. In the decades since its creation, KUCA has grown extensively and now has more than 75 students working on the station each semester. Students are able to pick what kind of program they would like to work or broadcast on, ranging from Top 40 songs to talk shows, like *Polo Gang Radio*. KUCA is funded through student fees and can be heard throughout Faulkner County.

The Ebony Singers were a gospel choir that formed on campus in 1977 with the purpose of increasing fellowship among students and to "give praises to God in song." The choir visited other campuses and churches upon invitation. Their goal was to do one on-campus concert per semester but they also participated in programs for Black Emphasis Month. The Ebony Singers performed at Arkansas Tech and around the state in Woodson, North Little Rock, Little Rock, Texarkana, Crossett, Marvell, Menifee, and Conway, as well as Southern Methodist University in Dallas, Texas.

Outreach and community service have long been facets of Greek life, and Phi Beta Sigma was no exception. In 1981, they donated a wheelchair to student health services. This type of act was fairly common among the Greeks, especially the National Pan-Hellenic Council, which hosted a variety of community projects.

1985 was the third consecutive year that UCA's student newspaper, *The Echo*, won the highest award, General Excellence, from the Arkansas College Publications Association (ACPA). The ACPA also named *The Echo* the all-American newspaper for the second year in a row and gave *The Echo* second place in photography, art, and graphics.

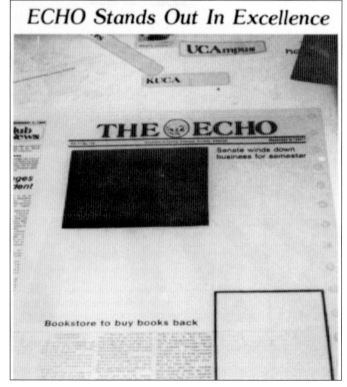

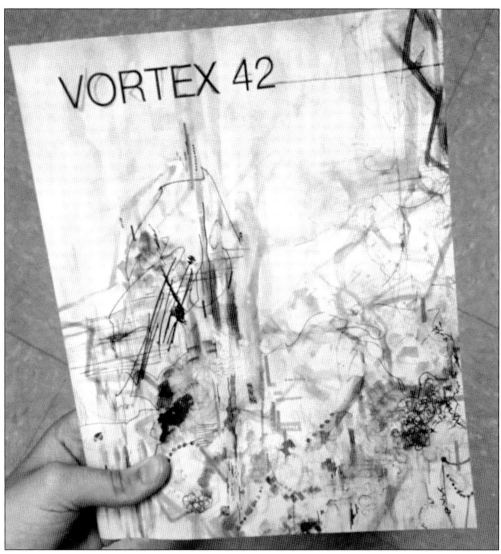

Vortex is a student-published literary magazine with pizzazz; it provides students the opportunity to showcase their creative work. The magazine is divided into two sections. The print section features stories, poems, photography, drawings, and paintings, whereas the online section provides access to videos, films, and documentaries. Submission applications for *Vortex* open each fall in October, and it is published every April. It also now produces a podcast. (Courtesy of *Vortex*.)

In the early 1990s, Gov. Bill Clinton's presidential run started the conversation of politics for students at UCA. The UCA-operated Channel 6 started *Arkansas Perspective* in 1993, which was a half-hour, weekly show that covered current events with top-elected state officials. *Arkansas Perspective* allowed students to be involved in the production and execution of broadcast journalism. Ernie Dumas hosted the show and was the former political and editorial writer for the *Arkansas Democrat-Gazette*. During local elections, students covered both Democratic and Republican headquarters in Conway.

The 1995 school year saw unprecedented student protests at UCA. When the board of trustees met over spring break, they agreed to increase tuition by the fall semester and to combine the geography, political science, and sociology departments. Both decisions were criticized by the student body, particularly after $400,000 was allocated to renovate the President's Home. After the board meeting, students felt their voices were being ignored and came together in a protest. The student activism led television networks and local news stations to cover the story and student concerns, creating a protest like none other in UCA's history.

UCA student ambassadors are chosen on a yearly basis from each department and regularly show incoming students the ropes around campus. High school groups often tour UCA on Bear Facts Day and are shown around by student ambassadors. Allowing current students to give campus tours allows potential students to ask honest questions and get an accurate understanding of life at UCA.

UCA's Greek community is always reaching out—in 1996, Delta Zeta member Libby Pledger encouraged a Special Olympian right before she competed.

"Greek Week" is a huge event that still takes place to this day. It started as a joint event for all the Greeks to come together to create bonds with each other, compete in games, and serve the community all in one big week. Here, two sorority sisters participate in one of the many fun activities during Greek Week in 1996.

During 1995's Greek Week, the organizations collectively raised $2,000 for D.A.R.E. (Drug Abuse Resistance Education), as well as hosted guest speakers that promoted AIDS awareness with the presentation, "Friendship in the age of AIDS." They also held a Twister competition!

Greek Week is not just about service because all work and no play makes for a dull Greek. There are themed parties at which fraternities turn their houses into tropical islands or use black lights to add a fun glow. Fraternities and sororities also partake in competitions, like the sack race, during Greek Week.

Another big part of Greek Week is the step show that typically happens at the end of the week, during which fraternities and sororities perform choreographed step routines.

P.R.I.S.M.
PRESENTS
UCA's DRAG SHOW

The PRISM (Pride, Raising Awareness, Involvement, Support, and Mentoring) Alliance was formed in 1997 to support LGBT students on campus. Because of the widespread criticism of the gay community, PRISM's primary goal was to be more open and active on campus in order to create a supportive community for gay and lesbian students. PRISM took an inclusive approach and kept no official roster but left all meetings and events open to everyone. By 2000, around 30 students subscribed to PRISM's email list, and 15 students were "stable members."

By 2009, UCA's PRISM Alliance had 80 regular members, including students, faculty, and staff. PRISM hosted a variety of events throughout the school year, most notably "Coming Out Day," where group members set up a door, representing a closet, with an information table in front of the UCA Student Center and provided fun activities like face painting. On Coming Out Day, members from a transgender group in Little Rock came to UCA in support of PRISM's effort.

Tau Beta Sigma and Kappa Kappa Psi are on-campus organizations for members of the Bear marching band who want to help give back to their community by working with local nonprofit agencies and sponsoring events. Pictured are the 2010 members.

In 2010, Ashley Hulsey served up pancakes at the annual Alpha Sigma Tau pancake breakfast, which continues to raise money for Alpha Sigma Tau's national philanthropic project: Pine Mountain Settlement School.

UCA's National Pan-Hellenic Council is stronger than ever. Pictured here from left to right are the 2014 council members, NiKendra Boston, Gabrielle Lee, Dennis Mattison, Portia Crawford, Jasmine Wilkins, Donnie Madden, and Charles Carter.

In 2016, UCA students got the opportunity to gaze at the stars from the observatory in the Lewis Science Center. They were especially excited to investigate a super moon eclipse, which has not happened since 1982 and will not happen again until 2033.

The UCA Theatre presented *The Liar* as their show for the 2016–2017 season. The plot follows a man who tricks two women into believing he has just returned from the Thirty Years' War, in which he claims he was instrumental. *The Liar* was the first of three student-run productions that year. This performance was bittersweet for many graduating students, as it was their last time to work with the UCA Theatre. Senior Sydney Stoner said she would not trade her "three years with the theatre for anything."

In 2015, UCA's Reynolds Performance Hall presented Broadway musical *The Addams Family* for a sold-out crowd. The *Log Cabin Democrat* hosted the event, which drew audience members from across the state. The classic story of *The Addams Family* illustrates that, regardless of how different people or families can look, they often struggle with the same problems as everyone else.

In April 2018, audiences flocked to *Avenue Q* in the Snow Fine Arts Center. The award-winning play is best described as "part Sesame Street, part comedy, and part musical." The main character, Princeton, is a college graduate who struggles to find his purpose after entering the real world. Students in the show said it had "a lot of heart," and it was "one of their best college experiences."

During the 2016 presidential election cycle, UCA's Campus Election Engagement Project (CEEP) partnered with Rock the Vote to engage students on campus with national politics. Students ran a two-day voter registration drive and started the semester with Rock the Vote week to inform students about both presidential candidates. CEEP hosted events that discussed how national issues would directly affect college students. CEEP was founded by Dr. Peter Mehl's Honors College Junior Seminar with hopes of making students aware and informed about the voting process and the importance of elections for citizens in a democracy.

Despite being over 100 years old, UCA's Greek life is still going strong, with new fraternities and sororities being chartered on campus every few years. Beta Upsilon Chi is one such fraternity. Chartered in 2009, the fraternity has all the typical staples of a traditional Greek group, but with an added focus on fostering a relationship with Christ. Another example of the way that Greek organizations are expanding into more diverse groups is Sigma Iota Alpha (pictured at the UCA Amigo Fest). This is a Latina sorority that came onto campus in 2017. A similar Latino fraternity, Phi Iota Alpha, was established the same year.

The biggest news in recent history regarding Greeks on the UCA campus was the announcement of a Greek Village. When completed, the new Greek Village will have houses for the larger sororities and fraternities, as well as ample meeting space for every Greek organization on UCA's campus.

UCA is home to the Mu Chapter of Phi Alpha Theta (the national history honors society). The Mu Chapter was formed in 1932. The organization's mission is to advance appreciation for historical inquiry, scholarship, and community engagement. The UCA chapter received the best chapter award in 2012 and 2013 under the guidance of Dr. Michael Rosenow and student president Laura Choate. The members who wrote and edited the current volume are picture from left to right: (foreground) Riley Kovalcheck, Chay McDaniel, Iain Montgomery, and Marcus Witcher; (background) George "Trace" Rhode, Emily Evans, and Jacalyn Pearce. (Vaughn Scribner is not pictured). (Courtesy of the Mu Chapter of Phi Alpha Theta at UCA.)

Three

SPORTS

Most adults would acknowledge that their years at college were full of dynamic change. A college student grows as a person, as a learner, and as a member of the world community during these first years away from home. However, many would agree that their most exciting collegiate memories center around sports. Students of the University of Central Arkansas are no different. Since the university's founding in 1907, UCA's athletic program has grown to 16 sports, giving young men and women from all over the globe an opportunity to come to the United States and receive a world-class education while playing for a loyal and enthusiastic fanbase. In this chapter, UCA alums will see faces they recognize, as well as some less prominent athletes, all of whom made their mark on UCA's athletic tradition. The chapter chronicles the iconic moments that were preserved forever through photography. The photographs compiled for this chapter are meant to help readers learn more about past UCA greats while enjoying their own piece of its collective story. Current students, lifelong Bears, and those new to the UCA community can wear their purple and gray with pride.

—Chay McDaniel and Iain Montgomery
undergraduates, History

The 1915–1916 Bears went 7-1 on the gridiron, with their only loss coming at the hands of Conway rival Hendrix College. The team credited their success to the leadership and experience of a core group of veteran players and to the work ethic instilled in them by legendary coach Dan Estes, pictured standing in the middle of the third row. Practicing six days a week, the 1916 squad became a well-oiled machine, rolling through one conference opponent after another.

ASTC halfback Bill Tiner breaks through Arkansas Tech's defensive line in what would become a 14-7 victory for the Arkansas State Teachers College. The 1962–1963 team ended their football season with a perfect 7-0 conference record and an Arkansas Intercollegiate Conference (AIC) championship—the first unshared AIC football title the school had held in 22 years.

Pushing his way through the defense, Terrell Dean rushes for a touchdown. Dean was part of the 1991 UCA Football team, the last team to play in the AIC before the Bears moved up to the National Collegiate Athletic Association (NCAA) Division II bracket. The Bears won their ninth consecutive conference championship in 1991, continuing a long history of excellence on the gridiron.

UCA's first president, John J. Doyne, tosses up a jump ball during a women's basketball game, around 1910. In their early days, the women's sports were known as the "Bearettes" and played on an outdoor court regularly. For reasons that remain unclear, women's basketball was discontinued from 1932 to 1976. Despite the lull, this photograph illustrates just how deep the roots of women's athletics are at UCA.

While the 1918–1919 school year was not a remarkably successful year for ASNS athletics, it marked a crucial moment in the school's history. With World War I coming to an end, students were finally able to return to school and continue their athletic careers. Coach Dan Estes also returned from his position as an Army lieutenant and, with his return, the men's athletic program was finally able to get back into its old rhythms. Though the men's basketball team only played two games during the 1918–1919 season, first winning against Morrilton and then losing against Hendrix, it was a pivotal season for the team, and, according to the school's yearbook, "marked the beginning of a new epoch in boys' athletics at the Normal School."

Under coach Cecil Garrison, the ASTC "Tutors," as they were known back then, went 14-6 during the 1953–1954 basketball season, including a big 82-78 win over Memphis Navy in the second game of the season. Pictured here, an ASTC player goes up for a jump shot as his teammates look on.

The 1984–1985 UCA women's basketball team, affectionately referred to as the "Sugar Bears," had an outstanding season. Under the leadership of Ronnie Marvel and Barry Lueders, the nationally ranked team had an outstanding 18-2-1 season record.

ASC's leading scorer, Conny Johnson, powers his way to the goal, gaining two more of what would be a 33-point game against Arkansas Tech. Though the Bears ended the season with a rather underwhelming 5-13 conference record, Johnson would achieve a record-setting 42-point game against the College of the Ozarks, finishing the season as the conference scoring champion with a 25-point average and being named to the All-AIC team.

UCA senior Scottie Pippen slams the ball through the net while his opponents from Monticello watch in awe. Averaging over 23 points and 10 rebounds per game, Pippen was one of the greatest, if not *the* greatest, players in the school's history, going on after his 1986–1987 season to be drafted by the Seattle SuperSonics, becoming the first UCA basketball player in history to go pro. Pippen would go on to become one of the most successful NBA players in history, being selected as a member of both the 1992 and 1996 USA Olympic "Dream Teams," attaining six NBA championships, and being recognized in 1996 as one of the "50 Greatest Players in NBA History."

In the midst of the golden age for baseball—America's pastime—UCA enjoyed great success on the diamond. Pictured are a few of the 1912 Normal Bears during bunting practice. Though the setting does not resemble the modern facilities surrounding collegiate baseball, this photograph illustrates baseball's roots as an everyday man's game, able to be played anywhere there are willing players.

Alan Humphries makes it safely to first base with the throw right behind him. Humphries was a pitcher on the 1972 baseball squad, a team that won its National Association of Intercollegiate Athletics (NAIA) district championship and finished runners-up at the regional tournament in Knoxville, Tennessee, finishing the season with 19 wins and 12 losses. Pitchers Dwight Duhart and Paul McGinnis were named to the All-AIC team in 1972.

Here are conference champions! Pictured are the four members of the 1954 ASTC 440-880-yard relay team who placed first in the AIC track championship. From left to right are Bill Kessinger, Allen Meadors, Steve McCulloch, and Don McConnaughey. Kessinger also won the 100-yard dash individually. In both events, the Bears finished just ahead of runners from Hendrix College and Arkansas Tech.

Pictured are the members of the 1959 ASTC track relay team. From top to bottom are Henry Hawk, Donald Owen, Larry Malone, and Bob Valentine. Heading into the 1959 track season, following nearly a decade of conference dominance, the future was uncertain as nearly half the team was made up of freshmen, and a new coach, Raymond Bright, had just taken over. Any doubt about the team's and coach's abilities quickly faded, however, as they went on to compete for the top spot in every event the team attended!

Truly an all-time Bear great, Gerald Cound won the 1962 Neil Martin Award, presented annually to the state's top athlete. During his two years at ASTC, Cound broke numerous track records, including the 880-yard run, and lettered in basketball, baseball, and track. He is considered to be one of the greatest track athletes in Arkansas history.

The 1969–1970 track team dominated the 1969 season, winning the AIC Track and Field Tournament for the first time in six years and having two of its members, David Johnston and Fred Jackson, named All-Americans, with Jackson claiming a 220-yard dash time of 20.9 seconds—the fastest time ever run by an Arkansas athlete.

Fred Jackson, seen here completing a warm-up run, had one of the best individual seasons in UCA sports history in 1970. Jackson set the AIC 440-yard dash record at 47.7 seconds, ran in the 880-yard team relay that set the 1:25.0 record, and placed fifth in the 220-yard dash at the NAIA National Track Championship in Billings, Montana. What a season, not to mention the six other record-breakers on the track squad that year!

UCA volleyball player Lisa Taylor jumps to defend her side of the court against Arkansas Tech. The Sugar Bears had a successful season in 1984, winning 14 regular season games and earning a berth in the NAIA tournament in Houston, Texas. Playing with speed and precision, they won their first game against Ouachita Baptist University before being eliminated, ending the season with a mark of 15-12.

Here are members of the 1984 UCA women's swim team. Finishing second in their conference championship, three swimmers went on to earn All-AIC honors. Tammy Casement of Hot Springs was an All-American swimmer the previous season, the first in UCA's history, and broke into the top-10 ranking of national swimmers in 1984. Casement (third from right) also set the fourth-fastest time on record for the 100 backstroke.

Warren Woodson coached football, basketball, and track at what was then called Arkansas State Teachers College, winning multiple championships in all three sports. In 1960, Woodson was the American Football Coaches Association's Coach of the Year. With more than 250 total victories, Woodson remains one of college football's most successful coaches of all time.

Propelling the Bears baseball team into a successful 1973 season, SCA Bear Gary Rhea hustles to first base in an AIC game. Though their regular season was definitely nothing to scoff at, the Bears' real success came in the NAIA District No. 17 Tournament, winning all of their games and bringing home the championship title.

The 1976–1977 UCA men's swim team had an impressive season, finishing third in the AIC meet with the strongest total points (65) in five years. On top of their impressive overall performance, UCA won five first places in the meet, more than any other team, with UCA senior and team captain Mike O'Brien setting a new AIC record for the 500-yard freestyle with a time of 5:18.611. The Bears also took three second places and one fourth place in the meet, proving themselves as serious competitors.

The Bears' football stadium, Estes Stadium, was opened in 1939 and was named after legendary coach Guy "Big Dan" Estes, who coached the Bears from 1915 to 1932. The field originally sported classic green grass, but in April 2011, UCA began the installation of purple and gray striped turf, making Estes Stadium the first college football stadium to have a striped field. The field remains as unique today as it was in 2011, being one of only eight college football venues using nontraditional field colors and one of only two schools with striped turf—the other being Lindenwood Stadium in Belleville, Illinois, who installed red and gray striped turf on their field in 2012.

Big Dan Estes taught aviation classes at UCA during World War II before dying of a heart attack in 1944. The UCA Athletics program has grown exponentially in the decades since his tenure, now offering football, basketball, baseball, golf, soccer, track and field, cross-country, tennis, and volleyball for both men and women.

At the beginning of the 2006–2007 season, UCA's women's soccer program moved up to Division I status. Every player was aware of the challenges, and nobody expected the season to be an easy one. Most preseason rankings had the team finishing near the bottom of the conference. Nonetheless, the team rose to the challenge and finished second in the Southland Conference with a record of 8-7! The team has continued to have success in Division I. Pictured, midfielder Jordan Slim attempts to avoid a challenge from a defender. The Bears finished the 2018 season with an impressive 16-4-1 record after falling to Abilene Christian in the Southland Conference Semifinals.

Four

OUTREACH

The University of Central Arkansas has a long history of providing students on campus the opportunity to reach out to the community of Conway, the state of Arkansas, and to countries and people around the globe. On campus, there are several organizations designed to connect with students, including those from underprivileged backgrounds. A major group on campus is the Division of Student Services and Institutional Diversity. They especially "seek to enhance interaction and understanding among diverse groups and cultivate enriched learning opportunities in a global community." Another major resource on campus is the Disability Resource Center. Extending beyond campus, many students and student organizations volunteer for community efforts. The university even has the Division of Outreach and Community Engagement. This division invites the community to get educated in person or online and in very specific areas, such as accounting fundamentals or Writeriffic: Creativity Training for Writers. The Division of Outreach and Community Engagement originally began as the extension department under the Arkansas State Normal School. In 2019, the division celebrated its 100th anniversary. Internationally, UCA has a broad representation of cultures and countries due to the care and interest in embracing global diversity. Programs for students include UCA students studying abroad at other universities and international students at UCA using the Intensive English Program. UCA partners with 27 universities around the world, ranging from distant Xi'an, China, to neighboring Guadalajara, Mexico. UCA also has an Office of International Engagement whose main goal is to, "[create] a supportive, diverse, and collaborative community on campus and in the greater area through cultural and educational programming." All these initiatives at UCA strive to educate others and unite different people together who, otherwise, would likely not be connected. The university encourages and instills a sense of service and engagement within students.

—Emily Evans
undergraduate, History

In 1978, UCA art students Susan Bauer and Judy Freidel assisted Dr. Jerry Poole, chair of the Department of Art, in painting a mural of Arkansas cultural history for the Little Rock Airport terminal.

Each year, UCA is able to bring in phenomenal speakers from across the country, and sometimes, even the world. During the fall 2000 semester, the university hosted Joseph Mutaboba, then Rwandan ambassador to the United Nations. He was the keynote speaker for the Umoja Wa Afrika, or the Unity of Africa in Swahili, which was a two-week-long event on campus.

In 2004, UCA students raised thousands of dollars for St. Jude Children's Research Hospital in Memphis, Tennessee, through the Up 'til Dawn event. The final theme centered on different decades throughout history, with each decade associated with activities and food. Students partied the night away with karaoke, sumo wrestling, a casino, and a dance.

UCA's Up 'til Dawn Chapter, born in 1999, was the second chapter in the nation. It is a student-run organization that is broken down into teams, which are each required to raise a certain amount of money. The money is raised through specific group or individual projects.

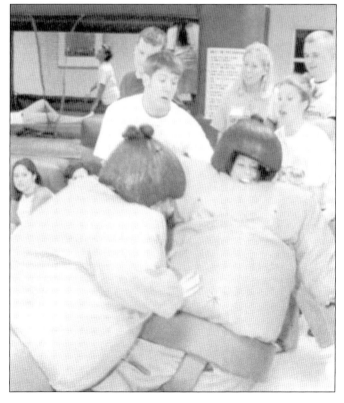

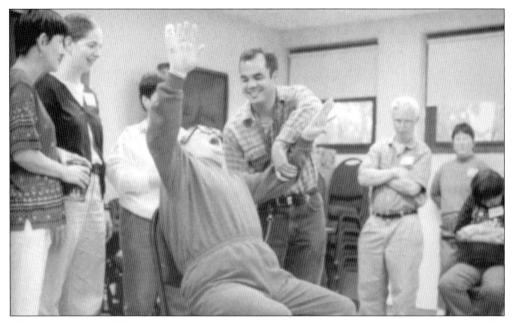

UCA's Occupational Therapy Program is well distinguished among other departments. The Acting Creates Therapeutic Success (ACTS) program is a major reason. This program is designed to provide performing arts opportunities to individuals with disabilities. The goal is to encourage them to do what society often believes they cannot. This collaboration takes place between the Department of Occupational Therapy and the UCA Theatre.

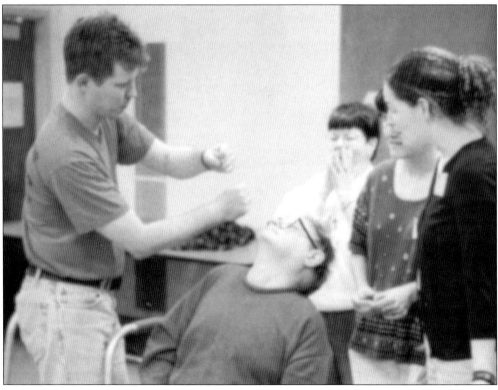

Following Hurricane Katrina in 2005, UCA and Conway communities reached out to those fleeing the wreckage in search of aid. Gulf Coast residents were provided temporary housing in various places across the city of Conway. UCA hosted 15 displaced students who were all offered and accepted in-state tuition to begin at the university. These students were given immediate assistance finding housing and putting together class schedules. UCA Greek life provided many services and fundraisers for the cause, including helping evacuated citizens fill out relief forms and collecting money throughout the city for those in need.

Always on the leading edge of technological advancement, UCA began offering digital filmmaking as a major in the College of Fine Arts and Communication in 2004. Dr. Brice Hutchinson (pictured) noted, "We are teaching something artistic while using the latest technology that allows students to get to work on a practical level."

As the 80 Proof peer education group demonstrates, drinking alcohol can be far more dangerous than fun. Every year, 80 Proof gives UCA students the chance to smash a clunker car for one minute (in exchange for $1). This helps fund outreach initiatives to educate college students on the dangers of alcohol consumption.

UCA Disability Support Services works to help include all students at the university. The goal of the office is to "maximize students' educational potential while helping him or her develop and maintain independence," according to its website. In 2008, the Disability Support Services moved to the Student Health Center, gaining more wheelchair room, testing rooms, and overall greater accessibility.

Every year, UCA's campus has an influx of international students from around the world. The university set up a campus organization called Team Global to help get international students acclimated to their new country and university. Not only does the university have a strong international student pull, but it also has a wide range of international faculty who help sponsor groups, like the Chinese Immersion Camp (pictured).

UCA students are always happy to help. In 2006, students lined up to donate blood to help with Hurricane Harvey. Many had never given blood before but found the perfect opportunity to do so at UCA.

Among the many departments at the university, the Department of Environmental Science is extremely active. This department is composed of several dedicated students and faculty desiring to serve the community. During March 2009, environmental science students took part in the northern snakehead eradication event. This event was necessary to stop the invasive species from devastating local ecosystems.

Several UCA students each year study abroad in countries around the world. Many students not only study a new culture but also volunteer at places of need in that country. Student Morgan Poole volunteered at a children's home called Casa Hogar Galilea when studying abroad in Monclova, Mexico. During her time there, she helped meet the physical, emotional, and spiritual needs of the children when their parents were unable.

UCA student ambassadors are the backbone of student-focused outreach efforts. They are paid to conduct a minimum of seven tours per semester (most do far more), and they are often seen walking backwards around campus with a group of eager students and parents in tow!

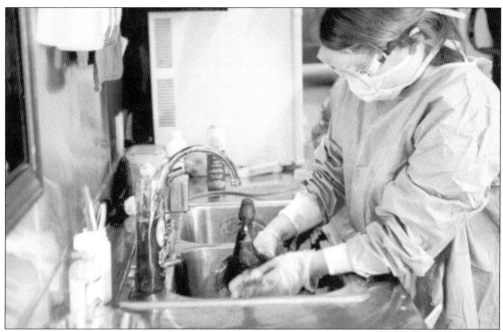

During March 2013, Exxon's Pegasus Pipeline burst in Mayflower, Arkansas. Within a week, UCA students, the biology department's Dr. Vickie McDonald, and the physics department's Debra Burris volunteered to help find and clean wildlife in the area of the oil spill. UCA's group of volunteers greatly aided in the search for hurt wildlife due to the wide range of the spill.

In 2007, UCA students created the Dee Brown Memorial Garden in honor of the famous American author who attended UCA in his youth. The garden features a fully edible landscape and sits behind Arkansas Hall (a residence hall). Students help operate the garden throughout the year.

The Arkansas Center for Research in Economics (ACRE) was founded in 2014. ACRE's main objective is to conduct economic research and to help improve Arkansas by introducing students, the public, and the legislature to the ideas of free enterprise. Each year, ACRE also runs student programs, including a speaker series and reading groups, where students engage with both historical and economic ideas. These and other programs provide UCA students with diverse perspectives about the ways in which economics affect all our lives. (Courtesy the Arkansas Center for Research in Economics.)

Over the years, UCA has had many veterans step into the classroom. UCA has also honored its veteran alumni with various memorials across campus. UCA constructed the World War II Memorial in 2003, and in 2016 it built the All Wars Memorial. The total number of memorials on campus is currently 50.

UCA's considerable number of international students lends itself to diverse cultures all around campus. Typically, individual groups choose to share their culture with the campus. In April 2015, Japanese and Korean students alike came together to throw a Japanese and Korean Spring Festival. The UCA Student Center Ballroom was full of informational tables on Japanese history, Korean pop, haiku, and more. There were multiple musical and dancing performances. The Japanese community of Conway also participated and donated traditional clothes for the event.

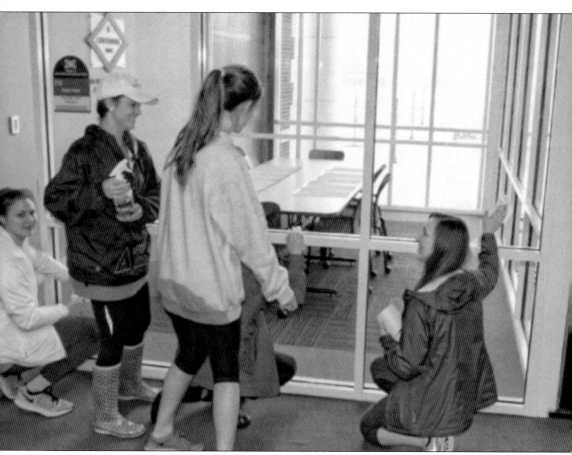
In 2017, the third annual Big Event was held at UCA. This is a campus-wide event that allows students to show support and aid for the local Conway community. Students began the day at 7:00 a.m. to start volunteering in the community. Volunteers do yard work, paint, and clean local homes, churches, or other public spaces. It is a designated time of year during which the students are able to show their gratitude for the community.

In November 2017, UCA's Muslim Student Association held a weeklong series of events called Islamic Week. The motivation behind the event was to educate UCA's student body along with Conway's community on Islam and unite people in the midst of international turmoil within the Muslim community. One of the main events held was titled "Get to Know Islam from Muslim not from Media," hosted by guest speaker Imam Arafat.

In 2017, UCA's College of Fine Arts and Communication created an event to commemorate the 60th anniversary of the desegregation of Central High School in Little Rock. This event centered around a 3-D projection-mapped video created by the film department, titled "If Buildings Could Talk." The video was projected onto the Central High School building on two separate evenings. UCA history students organized a bus tour with student guides at key locations. This commemorative event concluded at UCA Reynolds Performance Hall, which hosted eight of the Little Rock Nine students.

In 2017, Hurricane Harvey struck Texas. UCA's disaster response initiative, Bear Boots on the Ground, gathered 75 student volunteers to travel to the Houston area for disaster relief with the Southern Baptist Disaster Relief group. The work included going to houses to clear out wet debris in hopes of preventing mold growth so reconstruction on those houses could begin as soon as possible. The UCA delegation and Bear Boots on the Ground hoped to provide each family with a gift card to help restart their lives. A total of 35 houses were cleaned up by UCA with 1,500 volunteer hours put in by the students.

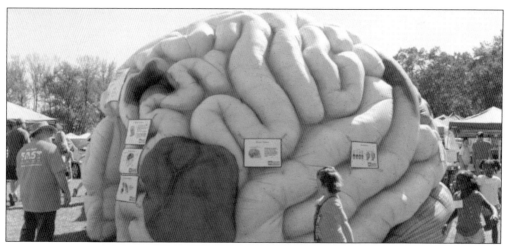

Each year, Conway hosts an Ecofest at Laurel Park to promote environmental awareness in the community. It is meant to be a fun, interactive, and educational opportunity for all who attend. A handful of UCA clubs participated in 2017, including the Student Dietetic Association, Food Recovery Network, UCA Geography Club, and Chapter of American Chemical Society. Many departments also set up displays.

During April 2018, UCA's Greek life and other students met together in the Farris Center on campus to honor and support Relay for Life and those who have and are battling cancer. The event consisted of games, food, and entertainment all for the benefit of cancer research. Many who had lost the fight to cancer were honored at the event with luminarias around the floor of the arena. The event ended with over $11,000 raised for Colleges Against Cancer.

One week each year, the National Pan-Hellenic Council (NPHC) reaches out to the students to introduce them to its organizations. The theme of 2018 was "NPHC: The Black Experience." The NPHC at UCA is composed of nine historically black fraternities and sororities, also known as "the Divine Nine." The main event of the week was the Unity Step, where members of different organizations stepped together and individually in front of Old Main.

Every year, UCA holds International Week in November to celebrate different cultures, honor the international students at the university, and give them the opportunity to share their traditions and customs. The university hosts roughly 600 international students, coming from over 70 different countries. Each day has a different focus to get students and staff involved to learn; one event that occurs is a passport drive, which aims to get students ready for international travel or study abroad.

The Office of Diversity hosted Amigo Fest in October 2017 to reach out to UCA's Latino community. Local restaurants, such as Las Delicias and Don Pepe's, supported the event by serving food, ice cream, and beverages. Entertainment was provided by Mariachi America and the Yumare Mexican Folkorico Dancers. The Office of Diversity previously held an Amigo Cup, which was a soccer cup for Conway's Latino community, but the fest was the better way for it to expand its reach. The event also doubled as a health fair with free health screenings. The event was sponsored by UCA's nursing students.

Discover Thousands of Local History Books
Featuring Millions of Vintage Images

Arcadia Publishing, the leading local history publisher in the United States, is committed to making history accessible and meaningful through publishing books that celebrate and preserve the heritage of America's people and places.

Find more books like this at
www.arcadiapublishing.com

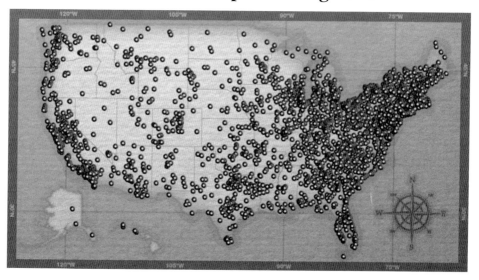

Search for your hometown history, your old stomping grounds, and even your favorite sports team.

Consistent with our mission to preserve history on a local level, this book was printed in South Carolina on American-made paper and manufactured entirely in the United States. Products carrying the accredited Forest Stewardship Council (FSC) label are printed on 100 percent FSC-certified paper.